BLACK ICE

Barry Butson

Black Moss Press
2000

Published by Black Moss Press, 2450 Byng Road, Windsor, Ontario, Canada N8W 3E8. Black Moss books are distributed in Canada and the U.S. by Firefly Books.

Black Moss would like to acknowledge the Canada Council for the Arts for its generous support of its publishing program. Funding was also provided this year by the Ontario Arts Council.

Canadian Cataloguing in Publication Data

Butson, Barry Curtis
    Black ice

Poems.
ISBN 0-88753-339-6

    1. Title.

PS8553.U76B56 2000   C811'.54   C00-900566-8
PR9199.3.B86B56 2000

Cover design by John Doherty. Cover photograph by Gabe Gervais.

ACKNOWLEDGMENTS

These poems have appeared, sometimes in slightly different versions or with different titles, in the following magazines and anthologies or on CBC Radio One's Out Front. The author wishes to express appreciation to the editors and producers.

Canada

The Canadian Author, The Canadian Forum, Firm NonCommittal, Ariel, The Antigonish Review, Descant, Losers First: Poems and Stories on Game and Sport, Contemporary Verse 2, Carousel, Prairie Fire, The Amethyst Review, Tower Poetry, Canadian Writers Journal, The Literary Network (e-zine)

The United States

Loonfeather, REAL, Touchstone, Midwest Poetry Review, Voices International, The Laurel Review, Conservative Review, Fox Cry, Plainsongs

The United Kingdom

Envoi, Iota, Poetry Review, Staple, Fire, Planet, Sepia

France

paris/atlantic

TABLE OF CONTENTS

Portraits

Anonymous   11

Jimmy   13

Al   14

White T-Shirts, Red Blood   15

One of the Simple Men   17

A Considerate Man   19

Handprints   20

That's Why She Never Wears Green   21

Couple in Black Bathing Suits   22

Saludos y Sonrisas   23

Still Life of Aging Athlete   25

Last Game   26

Hot Evenings

What was on my parents' dresser   31

The Babysitter's Loss   32

Boys   33

Sons as Monuments   34

Not Big Enough   35

Spirals   37

Excursion   39

Striking Out the Coach   42

Meltdown   43

Don't Write About Me   44

Night of Fire   46

Wild, Wild Life   48

Cooler Moments

What We Need   52

Power of Forgiveness   53

Southside Swimming Pool   55

Photo of the Whyte Packing Company Employees, 1955   57

I Kinda Wish   60

Dark Ladies of the Gyms   62

Can't Colour Love   63

Sex in a Raccoon Coat   64

We Have This   67

The Release of Autumn   68

Let's Just Say   70

Encroachment   71

Was That You, Jim?   72

Darkness and the Star

Before the Storm   76

Snow Days   77

On the Feast of Stephen   80

This One Day   81

Addicts in Green   82

Snow Tunnel to Compost Box   83

Black Ice   85

PORTRAITS

ANONYMOUS

I want a job with the CBC
talking softly in the afternoon
introducing classical music
that someone else has selected.
I want a script to follow
that someone else has written.
I do not want anyone on the subway
to know what I do for a living.
I do not want my face associated
with my occupation. Let them take me for
a store clerk or a streetcar driver.
I want my face free
to regard the world carefully
without the world
looking back.

If I cannot have this job with the CBC,
I want to be a dairy farmer,
and milk my cows in the dim light
and thin warmth of the barn,
filling a stainless steel tank
each day of my life with milk
that someone drinks without knowing
the face of the man who milked the cow.

If neither of these jobs is possible for me
I want to be a nightwatchman
in an art gallery who arrives after
everyone's gone home and goes before
the others come back to work.
I would not mind the portraits staring

at me in the darkened rooms; far better
that than my face hanging on a wall
for others to inspect   whetstone
on which they sharpen imaginations.

Let me be
      a voice over a wire
      a milker of my own cows
      a face outside the canvas

My heroes were Clark Kent and The Lone Ranger

JIMMY

Jimmy was a Chinese waiter
at the Golden Bamboo in Stratford,
where we all hung out, callous and poor,
but rich enough to slurp cherry cokes and
devour tin roof sundaes,
where a booth was all you needed
to feel right at home,
where I took a girl only once
and regretted it: all the guys
eyeing and jawing.

Jimmy was the most polite adult I ever met,
took so much guff
with a shrug and grin.   We laughed
at his shoes, so warped at the toes.
But Jimmy
was always there for us...
sad early or sad late, he was always working.
No woman had Jimmy that we knew of, acted
liked *we* were who he loved; Jimmy
for the Academy Award:

                              Best Actor as Waiter.

Jimmy, I admired you from a booth,
though you'll never know it
or care.

AL

Little man from down east,
a brush cut was good enough
for him, solitaire at noon hour
with a beer after
trying (not too hard)
to peddle
furniture all morning.

When Al was fed up
with pomposity - say
a suggestion too stiff
or meeting too mincing -
he would raise a hand
palm-outward and slash
it sideways in disgust,
blowing off, with slight exhale
from pursed lips,
the bullshit.

That gesture of Al's
was utter sanity - hardback chair amid plush chesterfields -
wisdom of The Little Guy
deciding.

Wasn't 40 when
his heart just said,
"piss on this"
and waved goodbye.

WHITE T-SHIRTS, RED BLOOD

As the man says, pound for pound
the toughest bastard in Stratford,

in his time.   Wounded three times
in Italy - either unlucky, stupid, brave, stubborn

or more likely too drunk to get out of the way -
he was awarded the Military Medal.

And the rest of his life was either anti-climax
or futile attempt to prove he deserved the award.

Mainly a long series of binges and bouts
in the city's hotel bars and alleyways.

He lived with his parents and I saw his dad
pulling gravel out of his back in the kitchen.

"Knocked me out and dragged me down an alley."
The next weekend he repaid the favour.

Worked as house painter and every morning
emerged in a fresh white T-shirt and knotted forearms,

Rolled home after midnight with blood in dots
and splotches - his and someone else's - ruining

the morning's promise. Flecks of the day's paint
might be mixed with red in a battler's idea

of a masterpiece. Tossed in favour of a new one
from the package of five he always bought at Woolworth's,

they were retrieved by his mother from the bedroom floor;
she soon stopped bothering to hold them up for inspection.

On weekends he strutted downtown in long-sleeved white,
shirts rolled just so many turns past his wrists.

A man of pride and vanity, if you jounced his chair
in passing his barroom table, he would stand up.

Hearing words too jaunty in way of apology,
he would smash in your face, if not prevented.

His brother tells of his final years, daughters
coming to his door to visit and him saying,

"What the fuck do youse want?" Not knowing
or caring who they were. Sluts from sluts in any case.

Still, he invited them in and they saw the glass jars...
every few feet, urine-filled. Since his legs were swollen

and the can was upstairs, he lined the jars right to the toilet door
and that way made it without pissing on the floor.

You can see why he survived the war and why
he won the MM.   His brother speaks of what

he might have been, with that medal boosting him post-war.
But there was the booze, always the booze,

right to the end. Taxis delivering it to the door,
where he on his thick legs answered in a T-shirt,

always white.

ONE OF THE SIMPLE MEN

It is summer   deep rich summer/so hot and humid outside
your balls sweat if you take two steps.
                        But I'm inside my apartment/where the air
conditioner hums its monotonous tune/the newspaper was waiting
in the hallway outside my door.

I am finished it now; Regis and Kathy Lee are gone
for the day/I think I should take the garbage down
to the dumpster in the parking lot. I think I can smell it
from where I sit/And there is nothing else to do/
I am completely free.

                        I am like all men who leave their families/
I am responsible only to myself/and I am very easy
to satisfy, needing only an assortment of diversions:
sports on tv, *Playboy* to read, a car to take on occasional
excursions, and the slightest hope that there is a woman
out there somewhere in the shining city who will call
or perhaps respond eagerly if I called   late and drunk.

I am one of the simple men/ one of the guys who shops
at the all-night A & P/ who needs all the laundry tips
he can get/and reads the tv guide thoroughly/ I am one
of the simple men/who like younger women/ and don't distinguish
much/ between nice ones and easy ones.

I don't shave on weekends unless I am going to see someone/
                        and usually I don't see anyone.
At nights I imagine hundreds of girls/who might be in my bed/
and they never turn down a request.

My neighbours don't bother me - though I sometimes hear laughter.

17

I am just one of the simple guys/they will never get to know.
What would we talk about anyway?

The cops sit outside my building looking for speeders
coming into town/ I sometimes watch them out my window/
they stop about two cars an hour/Most are driven by young men/
the kind I used to be.

No one can tell me what to do today/I am on vacation
from a shitty job you wouldn't want to do either/
And in a few more years I will be retired. Then
I will be truly free.

I love my wife and children/but they got too old.
I like things to be younger/maybe I'll get a kitten
for a couple years/or a pup.
                    Then I'll take them for a drive in the country
and get rid of them.

I think I'll go down to a doughnut store/have a coffee
and see who comes in. They're pretty casual in those places.

A CONSIDERATE MAN

All the fruit jars on his basement shelves
all the jars
were dusted and wiped clean - all
the peaches, plums and pears
he had preserved in the summer -
ready for the hands of survivors.
The muskrat traps were deliberately sprung
in the damp basement of the riverside house.

The oil tank beside the house was full,
thermostat set at 70.
Car had been sold, TV turned off.
All had been readied - will notarized,
debts paid, fruit jars wiped down recently
so our hands would not get dusty.
We even discovered in the work shed
his grave stone, personally engraved
with proper dates and ready to erect
beside his wife's homemade duplicate
in the community graveyard up the road.

The only thing he couldn't do for us
was wipe up his blood
from the kitchen's linoleum.
That wasn't too much for him to ask,
I think, this man who couldn't wait.

HANDPRINTS

The brotherhood of dirty paws
above a toilet in the men's room
of the sub shop
on the wall where we lean forward
to rest while using the urinal
makes me smile.
My brothers before me
left their mark and most are right-handed.

Leaning into the wall with one arm
is such a human yet barbaric act,
like a dog barking at footsteps
it cannot recognize.
Do not wash away those dirty prints;
let them work their way right into the wall
in a kind of niche where someday,
if this becomes the oldest sub shop in civilization,
small statues of men pissing may be set.

THAT'S WHY SHE NEVER WEARS GREEN

This is a tough woman...what woman isn't?
Anyway, she's tough and it got her to 80.

Tough rind, soft centre...that's Marg,
like some fruit that protects itself with thorns.

So many women I know are pineapples
like this...all exterior unless you get lucky.

Decades I've known her, but only yesterday learned
that she had four daughters, not three. One is my wife,

the secret one was Babes, who no doubt
had another name, but all her mother has told her

is that Babes died at six or seven months.
"How?" I ask, floundering in the quicksand

of female truths. "She was in her buggy on the porch
and there was a chemical fire in the neighborhood.

It got in her little lungs and she died a few weeks later."
I sit there at the kitchen table, staring at my wife.

Decades across this table and she never told me about her sister.
"That's why Mom never wears green.

She was wearing a green dress the day of the fire."
I just look at her and drink in the possibility

that maybe I do not know everything, after all.
Certainly not the many colours of women.

COUPLE IN BLACK BATHING SUITS

The sun paints across the waters a thick swath
so brilliantly scarlet you cannot look at it,
and the couple who just waded in for a last-minute swim
are mere silhouettes in the foreground.
                    They are frolicking.
He is a big man, wider than tall,
and so is she, but in the water
they are sleek seals.   Their heads close,
they hug and smooch,
dive and dunk.
He picks her up like a ballerina
and tosses her.
She gets onto his back
and wraps arms around his neck.
They are the only joy left in the world.

I walk away just before the sun sets,
leaving them out there.
I do not want to - even in the dusk - see
his hairy chest emerge,
her thick thighs marbled with veins.
Do not wish to see them on the sand,
watch them dry off into land mammals,
pop into a car, bump down its springs an inch,
drive off and move among us.
I want them in the lake,
disappearing soon in darkness.

SALUDOS Y SONRISAS

In the San Luis Potosi panaderia, a school girl
with forgettable features speaks quietly with her father
in the doorway of a busy hour.
He is very short to be a security guard,
but his uniform and billyclub declare that he is,
and for such a young girl to converse for so long
with a grown man means that he is also her father.

It is time to return to school so she moves off with waves and smiles,
but reluctantly, and makes her way through crowd of customers
to the cashier, who must be her mother or why would she also rate
a hugging goodbye?

The young girl leaves through one opening of the double doorway
in her green and red uniform, crosses the cobblestone calle
buzzing with Volkswagens thirty years old and green Nissan taxis
and just as she passes almost from view down a sidestreet,
she halts.

Turns, to look back at her plant-like father, her potted palm
of a father, who is now engaged in conversation with another man.
She can't catch his eye.

But will not leave until she does.
Late for school or not, she will wait.
Hand ready, eyes pointed like a dog's, she finally
is included in his world again as he raises his eyes from listening,
sees her waiting and waves with the sweetest smile a security guard
has ever bestowed on another human being. With this,
she waves back, smiles and disappears.
She is secure, happy; her place in the world
is beyond question - for her father adores her.

It may be that — had he not looked up
for many more minutes - she would have gone to school.
But I do not care to consider
such imperfect constructions.

STILL LIFE OF AGING ATHLETE

Sound asleep.
The fat old fart's head tilts
left as he dreams a midwinter siesta
fueled by a full day's work,
some chocolate cookies
and a bag of potato chips dipped
in a plastic "glass" of Canadian Club and 7Up
that sits empty on the edge of the tub.

His bare legs stretch out above the water's end,
each smooth on the outside as a Doberman's conscience
from rubbing against his woolen pants.
Beside the glass on tub edge rests - spine up - a TV guide
and a book he has tried to read about 37 times
since Christmas: two pages and he's comatose.

He dreams of days when he could still skate,
drive full-grown men into the boards, when
soft-skinned women used to call.
His sleep is so sound that when he awakes
he mutters a word or two of surprise
that he is in water once-warm and not
his bed. He blinks and squints in the bathroom light,
feeling lousy in the cool water; he knows what his dozing
means, but as yet is unwilling to pull the plug.
The fat old fart lies there,
perfectly still, not thrilled
to understand that all you leave behind
in this long, overtime game
is a grey line your dead skin
paints around a bathtub.

LAST GAME

Late November, courses deserted.
Pins put away.

Trees naked, the leaves squashed by rain onto the greens
like brown postage stamps.

Driving out here along country roads, I saw
hunter after hunter in well-placed stands
waiting for deer to come out of the woods for grain,
florescent-orange suits spaced every so many yards
in a gruesome grid of insurance salesmen and welders
that few deer would elude.

I tee off in afternoon mist,
two hours before dusk, just time for nine.
This may be the last game for a while.

A straight drive, as it often is this time of year.
Your game's at its best but the season's over,
most guys already curling....hunting.
I like the course pinless and empty, partly just to have it to myself
and play at my own pace.
There's also this gloom hanging over the world -
hickory nuts on the ground with husks splitting open,
milkweed pods long burst, grass dormant
but soft enough to lie down on for the winter,
corn fields along number ten already harvested.
Nothing left for the land to do except get under the snow for five months.

When I get to my ball, I can barely see the elevated green.
I know it's about 160, though, so I take a six iron
and ride it into the mist.
By the feel of it, should be close.

Where were these swings in the year-end tournaments of my life?

I'm taking each step, making each stroke with deliberation,
moving as slowly as I ever have, stopping right now for instance to listen
to a small flock of geese invisible overhead.
They're going somewhere I'm not.
I'm right where I want to be.   Why, I'm not sure.
It isn't the golf so much as need to be out here
in the final temperate days of the year
on fairways once fields where you can still step
into the bush and see cane and bracken turning blue,
vines thick enough to sit on if you're weary,
Poor Tom cloisters where small birds spend winters.

The bag feels light on my left shoulder.
Don't hit the two iron well, so I left it in the trunk.
Along number twelve I drop the bag,
walk into the woods to piss and imagine gun-shots, deer dying,
but really just hear the distant roar of machinery and, downwind,
I can smell pig manure being spread. These are the last days
in this climate to be human or vegetable; soon we will wrap
our shrubs and selves in burlap.
It's a long winter to get through:
freezing rain, blizzards, plugged laneways,
whiteouts and black ice, candles and coal-oil lamps.
Snow-belt winters, lake-effect miasma.
Storms will bury these fairways in snow nine-iron deep,
alabaster drifts sloped and shaped by north-west winds.
I could lie down in this bush with the birds and hares
and be perfectly happy living on bark and snow melt.
But I've got some bloody holes to finish first.

Below number thirteen a quail whirrs up at my feet
and I laugh out loud. She thought she'd be undisturbed
by golfers this late in November. I really could stay here forever.

The par-five fifteenth drops off into bush all along
the right-hand side that no-one ventures into
because of its steep slope. I like to think of this bush
as virgin territory, a retreat I can always use
if the worse someday happens.
Right now, conditions are far from that stage
but you never know - things happen quickly.
Birdie one hole, double bogie the next...

As I march along, I hate the thought of losing
this personal garden that once was just farmer's field,
hills and ponds, but now is perfect combination
of groomed grass and the threat of wild dogs.
On the other hand, the sun's close to setting.
You can feel the new cold coming quickly.

After I hole the final putt, I would kind of like
to walk back down the eighteenth fairway
and then the next and next
so I can for a while longer postpone
those five months of dry houses, couches and worse.

But no
        ...it's over.
Long winter coming.

HOT EVENINGS

What Was On My Parents' Dresser

It lowered my spirits daily
to pass that room
on the second floor of my childhood house;
it frightened my bones nightly
in ghostly dreams
to envision the photograph
on my parents' dresser in the room where
- I had not before thought of this -
I suppose I was ill-conceived.

It was the picture of my sister, Myrna,
in her tiny coffin.

Born and dead before I
made my appearance (perhaps
in substitution for her), Myrna
reigned in the upstairs of our house.
Why must they remind me of their loss?
I sometimes wondered.

Maybe they expected me to learn from it,
but more likely they were devastated
by her snowflake departure.
Whatever.

How could I compete with that?
Every day, every night
they worshiped from their bed an angel.
Down the hall
the sorry replacement,
sweating.

THE BABYSITTER'S LOSS

Dad on his way to the hospital
with little blue Myrna
in his arms
stops
on the porch where
my older sister Junie is sitting
to show her Myna for the last time
alive   "because I used to babysit her,
I guess."

Junie tells me this now
decades later
                    tells me the brother
who never knew one of his sisters

or that the other held pain
like a crystal locket.

BOYS

The youngest sees mother axed
by the hired hand in humid weather,
father in the field
brothers at school,
tornado on the way.
He too is attacked
before the madman slits
in cowardice his own
wrists, but
the boy survives...sort of.   What

I find interesting and not
for purely academic reasons
is how that boy "turns out" -

his own school years
            the geography of bloody floors
            the history of the time it takes
            for a husband to come in for lunch
            the arithmetic of missed breakfasts
his adolescence
            the pimples of scream
            the romance of sodomy
            the prom of axe handles
his manhood
            the career of you're lates
            the wife of please don'ts
            the son of where's grandma

Will boys be any softer
  than the head of an axe?

Sons As Monuments

I wept when the black man told the white man
he did not have to chain himself
to the store his dead father
had operated with so much love
and which was about to be razed.
"This building isn't your father's monument,"
said the black man.
"You are."   I wept

                because I am not
a proud monument to my father,
never knew
I had to be.

But now   knowing
I understand that I have fallen far short,
must have
otherwise   why
would I have cried
when I heard those maudlin lines of a tv script?

No monument, Dad,
maybe I'm just the book
you could have written.
Maybe your other sons stand
as stony tributes to your life.
I am just paper,

  you old ghostwriter.

Not Big Enough

I'm not big enough to wring out a towel
not big enough to hold the prize show birds
and dip them in the copper tubs
like my father with his big arms in rolled-up sleeves
not big enough to sleep out in a tent
not big enough to have a .22
and shoot rats, not big
enough to reach the throat
of the rooster trussed-up by a leg to binder twine
not nearly big enough to enter the body
of Christ or my plump cousin
not big enough for man's work.

But I'm too big for my mother
to come and sleep with me anymore
too big to cry
too big to make mistakes
like dropping the towel in bath water
and not wringing it dry
too big for hugs
too big for women's work.

My job is to get the three oval tubs ready
with water just the right temperature for christening
prize show birds in the soapy one first, then the bluing,
then the rinse   my job is
to put the wire cages out on the lawn
my job is to pluck the scalded feathers
and pull out the guts
and wrap them in newspaper
my job is to eat a chicken every Sunday,
heart, liver, gizzard and all

my job is to leave my cousin alone
my job is to stop asking about guns
and how tall I'll be when I get
to slit the rooster's throat
my job is not to watch my sisters undress
I'm too big, not big enough
  for that.

SPIRALS

Spirals of Spirea, a bush of white blossoms hugging my childhood porches

          capturing my rubber balls in its stiff stems, like mean neigh-
bors.

Spirals of the hand and wrist snapping tobacco leaves in early morning
wetness

          three leaves at a time, backs breaking
as bodies become machines of

          spiral snaps, row upon row. Gathering

leaves to print dark stains on

          fingers teeth lungs

Spirals on the ice   she skates

          like a sewer, stitching circles around
and
around and around, learning

          her figures in the frost oval arena

Spirals of telephone cord carrying

          your voice to my ear, sifting the sand
of my
dreams, safely in your own room

          the spiral cord limp between us
your words so daring but so far away

          that your hands have scissors in them,
ready to
snip if I suggest

          a love more substantial

Spirals in space as a satellite is tossed

          to spin in sustaining orbit above us

and beneath us and forever a star

                        seed of our technology, sperm of our
science,
echo of interstellar erection

                        Spirals we climb of wrought iron
from earth's lowly basement
                        casements we slowly ascend to heav-
en
each turn losing sight of what's below
                        each turn a step towards peace,
muffled with mercy from the cries of earth
                        and rivers pounding to the seas

And spirals of light made by children with sparklers
                        on a warm night in May
the most innocent of designs
                        branding the night sky as they move
in romps across the lawn
                        showing the universe this light from afar
these tiny sparks of life way out here
                        in another galaxy
            children with sparklers
                        carving their names with leaps
                into the black of forever
                  valentines from earth
            to the masked men
                in the moon.

EXCURSION

Oh, I loved all things about it.

Being roused at 4:30 by older brothers,

the dark walk on summer streets

to train station a mile away.

Stomach and bowels churning.

Brothers re-visiting the prowls of last night,

farting and laughing.

Boarding and finding a seat, surrounded

by the people of the city, mostly adults, who had also decided

to spend a Saturday in Detroit.

We were Canadians from a small city;

Detroit was the big leagues. The big nation next door.

My brothers and I, of course, were heading

for Briggs Stadium, corner of Michigan and Trumbull.

Tigers against Yankees, or Red Sox some years.

Mantle at the start, or Williams at the end of amazing careers.

Al Kaline for Detroit, and Rocky Colavito before he was traded

so sadly away.

Just being on a train - the motion of rolling through backyards of towns

where out the window you saw laundry and lawn chairs of people

you'd never otherwise know.   Dogs

just-for-a-second-thinking of chasing us, but

instead standing straight-legged in awe at passing thunder.

Embarking at Detroit after bridging the river,
cursory check through Customs, then heading up Michigan Ave.,
lined on one side with pawn shops, the other with bars.
Going in, only ten, with drinking age brothers,
kid in the darkness of noon-hour sin, soles of my shoes in sawdust
of saloon floors, afraid to look at the strange black men
who laughed so loud nearby and wore orange slacks
and purple shirts and slanted fedoras.   Happy
to be pushed out the door by late-boozing brothers
into the brilliance of a street so wide and busy with cars and
walkers also hustling for the stadium and first inning.

Coming into view now, its silver-painted girders
like a spaceship, banks of lights turned on even in daytime.
Once inside, steel became grass, so emerald
and so diamond, the infield dirt almost orange.
Never saw anything like this before.
And there they were, all your heroes -
          that actually was Hal Newhouser
jogging along the track. His uniform number said so,
according to your program. Imagine that!
Hal Newhouser just jogged past you.   Keep looking.
There's Kaline, yep no doubt about it.
Al Kaline is taking batting practice.
Maybe he'll clear the roof.
It's all too much.

Then the ebb and flow of the game itself.
Hot-dogs and soft drinks, peanuts you can shell
and just drop the husks at your feet.
A sip of American beer from your brother's cup.
Mantle actually clearing the right field roof,
hitting it out onto the street. Imagine being out there

40

and this ball drops from the sky at your feet.

The trip home, tired. The people who went to Boblo Island
or elsewhere are drunk and between cars you see
a woman holding a man's jacket behind his bum
as he jabs her with his hips.   Her face.
Not even seeing you.
You hurry past and say nothing
to your brothers.

Sometimes fights, everyone whipped from their day.
The fun's almost over. Back to Stratford,
back to small conflicts, smaller hopes, drab dreams.
Someone pulls the emergency cord that runs
along the tops of the cars and the train screeches
to a long stop.   Conductor furious
quizzes the adults - "who done it, you bastards?"
I know, but would never tell.

The train slowly picks up steam and takes us
the rest of the way. By then, I'm asleep
and possibly dreaming.

STRIKING OUT THE COACH

My coach was drunk
and at the beginning of practice grabbed
a bat when I was on the mound
and bet me I couldn't strike him out.

I don't think Bill every thought of me
as a real athlete. Maybe
I was too good in school,
but for whatever reason
he thought at age 40 he could
hit something off the arm
of a skinny kid half his age.

I was real smart.
I struck him out
in three pitches,
throwing my best stuff
with concentration
I reserved for top hitters.
I struck out and humiliated
a guy who was drunk
and who spent several years
coaching me and my friends
in both baseball and hockey.

I took great pleasure in winning
and that, unfortunately,
was about the only thing Bill
liked about me
and the thing now
I like least.

Bill, too late, I apologize.

MELTDOWN

For her touch
        I burn with desire
and at night
        I glow
            as I walk in the park;
in daylight
        I avoid gasoline.

Once I took seven cold showers
        yet singed the towel
when I dried off, thinking of her face.

I'm afraid if she ever gave in
        and let me hold her in my arms
        she'd melt like caramel
and I'd be
        in one helluva
sticky situation.

Don't Write About Me

She said
don't write about me
in your lousy poems
I don't want to see myself spread
across the country naked
and stupid
the way a guy like you'd
centrefold me.

Au contraire, I told her,
tell her here, on paper.
I would surely write you gently,
slipping only the smallest word
between your sturdy legs,
never pulling out that long hard one
you so achingly fear.
I would remember my manners
writing about one so vulnerable
and sensitive as you.
No words would I put into your mouth,
not even "penis"; no hired-gun words
to challenge you at high noon
and in public about your secrets,
like how you dump your brat's diapers
or what you called your then-husband
in front of all your friends and me.

No, these words won't rape you
or even slap your sullen face.
I won't tell how you jumped
into my Camaro and like a lottery winner
announced you had no pants on
under your skirt.

Don't write about you in my poems?
I'll tell you what -
I won't write about you,
if you swear on a copy of *Cosmo*
not to tell anyone that once
I loved you.

Night Of Fire

Pascal burned with primal certainty.
Satisfied and purged from two hours' pain,
he inked it into parchment and
sewed it into a garment he wore every day.
Such is our consumption of earthly delights
that it took this constant reminder
to recall even the torture of two hours with God.

My night of fire lasted almost as long,
on the pay phone of the country club
with a hot mistress in humid weather.
She begged me to come over, told me
what she would and wouldn't be wearing,
what parts of her body I would enjoy.
It was the moon, she was manic.
Nothing would do but to have me.
Tired from tennis and sweating,
I was reluctant.
As man after man passed me
on their way to the john, they
knew as clearly as the click
of their spikes on the tile floor
what I was sweating about.
I was Bosch's wayfarer
denying the woman at the window,
in exile from my flesh.   Still,
I imagined the drive over
opening her screen door
seeing her diaphanous nightgown and under it
the lovely pudding of her flesh.
She was using every word
a woman can use on a man

who isn't there
to bring him quick.
Shall I repeat these words?

I let her suck on my "no's"
like peppermints
until she was ready to swallow
defeat. Some men by then
had passed me several times.
It was a hot night for drinking.
The urinals were full and stinking.
The telephone was sticking
like gum to my ear, her words like
the ends of a lily's stamens.
She burned up the lines for two hours,
my legs aching as I stood like a Brabant stork,
shifting from one court shoe to the other.
The men were disgusted in passing
She was disgusted in pleading
You are disgusted in hearing

But somewhere my god
was pouring on the heat of resistance
and forging for me a fate
slightly less sensuous.
I waited her out, won six to love
and even got my coin back
when she hung up.

I carry it always
like the parchment of Pascal.

WILD, WILD LIFE

Check it in, check it out.
Twenty bucks an hour, rent a room
Saturday afternoon in the sweet Fall
and football is on the tube while we're on the bed
comparing bodies. You shouldn't, but you tell me
your latest child isn't your husband's.
I shouldn't, but I throw you out of the room.
Wild, wild life.

I walk a lion through the snow of suburban streets,
bring him right into your house where your children sleep
and as you kiss me you feed him Oreos.
Wild, wild life.
I pray for snow to erase the footprints in your driveway.

I package my poems in a brown envelope
and as you stand there in front of your classroom
hand it to you, saying - "careful, there's a bomb
in there." Afterwards, you say, "when I opened it
I just started shaking."   Yeah,
real passion in French class.
Wild, wild life.

You tell me between corn rows, "I like it when
you talk dirty." I rip a cob off its stalk, shuck its leaves
and hold it like a knife.
"I'm gonna Faulkner you," I say. Inching
towards your soft spread of body. Giggling,
you enfold the wild, wild life.

I dunno, I'm a good boy who just would rather
be bad, scalding many a friendly folk with boiling looks
and evil books. I'm a guy who should be banned
from Vegas or Corinth for loving too much
the wild, wild life.   Check it in, check it out.

COOLER MOMENTS

What We Need

An old Volkswagen camper van
a compact War-time house with asbestos siding
patio out back
a pet named Sunny
two jobs of great simplicity
opportunities to gamble small and win big
who cares about the odds?
politicians to bitch at
several tv sets
a convenience store that's conveniently close
and open 24 hrs.
our own doughnut hangout
smokes and beer enough
golf clubs and carts
a pet named Sunny
two pairs of jeans apiece
T-shirts and ball caps with funny things
printed on them, like
Toronto Maple Leafs   or
Existence Precedes Essence
plastic garbage bags
two cars
security system
coffeemaker
Medicare
soap
            ourselves, just you and me, baby
plus Sunny
and
maybe
a gun

POWER OF FORGIVENESS

I am very attracted to the dignified
lifestyle of our Amish brethren,
are you?   I admire their focus,
discipline, restraint and spiritual strength.
I am glad they are among us, in pockets
of countryside where signs along the roads
warn: Caution, Slow-Moving Vehicles.
That means buggies, horse-drawn and filled
with people, real people in black and white dress,
straw hats or bonnets on heads sometimes bearded.
I am glad Corporate Canada and The Global Village
have not pulled all the dolphins and people up
in their nets.

       ****

Callow youths from families like ours with no
equivalent moral values threw a full beer bottle
into one of these buggies near Milverton
as they passed it in the opposite direction:
        buggy coming from church and heading home,
        car going straight to rust and hellery. The bottle
        struck Mary Kuepfer straight in her face, exploding
        like a grenade among smiles and dimples.
        She was taken by buggy to the hospital
        where 56 stitches sewed up the horror.
        In the paper, her photographed face did not look
        like that of a twenty-year-old woman; it looked
        like the Hallowe'en mask of a monster, but
        behind the thread-dark stitches she smiled.
        And when interviewed, she told the incredulous
        reporter that she forgave her attackers, just
        as she had been taught to turn her cheek.

The Amish carry no medical insurance, so
a fund was started up and money flowed
in response, not just to her pain,
but mainly that forgiveness she contained.

We were so happy she didn't blame us.

SOUTHSIDE SWIMMING POOL

Noonhour swim and sauna.
As the women absorb lessons like sponges,
the men perch like vultures in the sauna,
waiting to tear into their lengths.
Body-conscious, but mostly white & plump
as snowberries, they complain
about the women going over-time
and the boys
who (allegedly) hold pissing contests
to see who can hit the sauna rocks
from the farthest corner.
One says, "I'd take their dicks
and stick 'em to the rocks.
That'd cure 'em."

When the women decide to leave
the pool and drip into the sauna,
full of talk as a radio,
the men slink out and slip into
the water like bald otters.

Two of the oldest, in the deep end,
tread water facing each other
for conversation so quiet
no-one else can hear; these red-faced
fatsos could be plotting murder
or mergers, or just reminiscing
about when they both wore suits this time of day
and insulted inferiors for fun;
their blue predator's eyes are wary
of my non-member dog-paddling;
all men of the pool are sharks.

Such warmth in here on a winter's day,
such succulent steam and mellowing moisture;
I look from my point in the deep end
through the glass sides of the indoor pool
onto the snow-covered pines
and conclude:

> we can build paradise,
>
> but then the people move in.

Photo Of The Whyte Packing Company Employees, 1955

Seven rows of them
a couple dozen to a row
lined up outside the brick plant
where they spent nine or ten hours a day,
they are tiny in black and white newsprint.
Their names are listed below,
with some _____s because
the photo's owner has forgotten
or never knew them. Invitation
to identify these unknowns is extended
to readers.   I scan the faces and names
without hope of knowing many; they are older -
I was only a child when the photo was taken.
But I see the name then spot the upper body
of my old baseball coach, Cliff Palmer,
his ever-present suspenders showing clearly.
I shared years of glory with him, but never
knew where he worked. There is his youngest son too,
his dad got him a job...for a while.
Most of the women wear dresses and smiles.
Even the men seem cheerful this day.

Here are all the Stratford surnames -
English Sproat's, Scottish Leith's,
Irish Fitzgerald's, German Zimmer's.
Some of these people will still
be hanging on to their sixties
and maybe still working...somewhere.
But not here:
                    like all our factories, this one
is gone   and with it, the big families

of workers I so admired as a boy walking past
these brick dinosaurs on the way to school.
Families of small-city people
with a year or two of high school
who quit to work for forty years
or more at the same machine,
who never left town as I did,
but stayed among friends,
raised their own families.

We will never have these people again,
nor small cities where - when you went to the arena
or church - you could count on seeing fellow workers
and saying a few words to them.
All the furniture factories of Stratford,
Swift's poultry slaughterhouse,
the sprawling CNR shops, all these
generous employers are out of business,
shut down, their brick walls demolished.
Drive around town and see the fallen shells, faded
For Sale signs lining the perimeters of their lots.
School children are taken to the plywood fences
that surround them and told to paint suns and skies
and other cheerful designs on the plywood
so everyone can ignore history.

Most of the people in the photos are dead
or living on little, and many
of their children are unemployed or facing
pay cuts or job loss. Nothing is certain
now, but when these plants were running,
small cities ran like Swiss watches.
Everyone worked, the kids had games to play

and places to play them, the schools were full
of good teachers. No one worried
about tourism. They just did their jobs,
avoided mistakes and accepted low pay without unions,
or sometimes didn't.
Like these Whyte Packing Company workers
who pose for a picture with the boss,
Mr. Whyte himself, seated front row centre,
surrounded by family of sorts.

I Kinda Wish

I kind of wish I was seventeen
driving my dad's old Dodge, parked now
in the sun in front of Jane's house,
my left arm naked and lying along
the edge of the door, window down and
Jane leaning in to talk, with
the tips of her hair touching
the tanned nerve-endings of my lust.

I wouldn't mind at all her mindless
chatter as I stare down the street
and concentrate on her dark hair moving
back and forth along my arm
as she tempts me with all the instincts
of a sixteen-year-old female of the species - knowing
full well she is risking nothing
nothing at all   so long
as she is still outside the car
the car that isn't even my own.
Back and forth she sways her head,
poking it occasionally inside to lick
my ear, or peck at my lips.
I keep my eyes straight ahead
where her twin sister, Joan, sits sullenly on the left fender
in short-shorts, a perfect ass slightly bulging under her weight.
There are complex games being played.
Joan does not like me.
I want Jane in the car.
Jane only wants to keep the other two happy,
so she flirts with her feet firmly on the sidewalk.

When Joan eventually sighs loudly,

slides off the fender and stomps towards their house,
Jane will pull my head toward her,
kiss me once with meaning,
then run loyally after Joan. They're twins.

I will sit like a corpse behind the wheel, curbed again
but willing to wait for the epilogue:
                  when Jane will appear upstairs
in their bedroom window facing the street,
spread wide the sashes
and wave smilingly down at my eyes,
like some Juliet of St.Vincent St.

Only then will I turn the key
and drive off thinking
that wasn't bad
but I kinda wish
I was older and had a car of my own
and Jane would get in
and ...

It all eventually happened
... what I kinda wished for.
But now I sometimes feel
I would prefer to be that manipulated boy
who had to be happy
with merely a brush of some very clever twin's
pendulous locks.

DARK LADIES OF THE GYMS

Dark days of "Eddie My Love" soak my mind.
Memory is a blotter absorbing me back
to the dances in gyms so dim you couldn't see
the eyes of the girl who turned you down.

Cave days of torment and lust.
You would have gladly married
the first girl who touched you.
I would like a second chance.

Return and see them lined against the opposite wall
like your entire **future** in various dresses.
Every life they opened up
seemed to have satin crinolines.

Revive them to their sullen or good-natured youth,
petulance or purity. I would never take advantage,
remain shy and stupid about women's ways.
Wouldn't be six feet and handsome.
Would simply watch them lined up again
waiting for godknowswhat,
certainly not me.

Would assure them all
that things would lighten up...
they would not have to stand in the dark forever,
though the dances would, sadly,
end.

Can't Colour Love

Six a.m. and just light;
my wife's head sticks out
of covers on the pillow beside me.
Her thick hair is mostly grey.
Grey as fieldstone.
She has let it go
grey; she is
that kind of woman.
Will let it go white too
I imagine.

As young man at Saturday dance
breathing the auburn of her locks
I never dreamt I would want
a grey-haired lover.
As older man in a Sunday-warm bed
I know
love has no colour.
Even white
will more than suffice.

SEX IN A RACCOON COAT

When he & his wife were younger
with several small kids and lived
in a northern town, so busy
he never had time for poetry or
sensitivity towards animals...
in short, when he was more of a normal man,
he did something unusual...
drove all the way to Toronto one December Sunday
to a Hungarian furrier's in Chinatown where the Lord's Day Act
was being blatantly defied
and bought his wife a fur coat for Christmas.
He had no idea of her size and needed the help
of some female clerks to model the coat
and even put it on himself, since his wife
was not much smaller. He looked over
quite a few coats, like a wholesaler ranking
a trapper's offerings, before he picked out
one with fine lines and markings. Fur coats
were expensive then and by no means regarded
as verboten, especially in small northern towns.
It cost him two months' wages, but he bought it.

Back home, he took it to a friend's house
and asked the wife to store it somewhere until
Christmas Eve. She happily agreed and was astounded
that he would undertake such a daring feat. (Her
marriage wasn't the only one to later break up
over just such matters as husbands *not* going to Toronto
to pick out furs for their wives.)

On Christmas morning his wife slipped it on over her flannelette
nightgown and her photograph is right there in their album,

her wide smile showing a model's sense of
"ain't I special?"
That winter she wore it to staff parties,
she wore it to church,
she even wore it to hockey arenas.
It fit perfectly.
In the Spring she took it to a local furrier
and had it placed in cold storage.

The next winter
every time he saw it in their bedroom closet
the thought would come to him that wouldn't it be nice
if she stripped naked, slipped on the raccoon fur
and lay flat on her back in bed.
He visualized her in it, buttons undone,
maybe in high heels too.
It would be good.

But he couldn't ask her; she wasn't
the type who went for kinky sex.
He knew some women who might,
but not his wife.

* * *

Eventually, as we know, it was determined
that wearing fur coats was in poor taste, displaying
a politically incorrect blindness to animals' suffering. So
his wife stopped wearing the coat, and he
himself took to giving up whole weekends
to help build half-way houses for orphaned urban raccoons,
drove them even farther north in the Fall to release them
into Nature, fattened and fully ready to breed.
His wife stopped storing the coat over the summers
and it hung in the bedroom closet of one of their grown children,

losing more of its sheen every year.
He never thought about that trip to Toronto any more, never
considered asking her to put on the coat
now that they had the house to themselves and could
chase one another screaming from bedroom to bedroom,
her in fur and him quoting passages from the Marquis de Sade
or one of the Brownings at the top of his voice.

      He went to bed early and didn't snore;
    she went much later and did.

The coat just hangs there.

WE HAVE THIS

I'm trying to laugh with a mouth full of caramel
at this gypsy life in suburbia.   Walking with

the woman who knows me down to Zellers
on a nearly-warm Saturday evening, picking

up in the friendly wine nook two bottles
and seeing the new sign - "Now Open Sundays".

Feeling much better about this little life
as we walk back home down harmless

streets with other weekend people
so happy none would ever lay a finger

on our serenity, I'm thinking. Maybe
after a certain stretch of years you earn this:

money left over for wine, weather
warming, the world around you easy.

What is definite is the utter joy
of having someone sweet to walk with.

I think a game is on the tube tonight
in this gentle gypsy life of ours.

Get the glasses and pour the cheap rosé.
If we want, we'll order pizza later

and with each juice-spurting bite we'll count
the blessing of health enough to be able to walk

to Zellers and the arrival of the first Spring nights.
For a little while yet, we have this.

THE RELEASE OF AUTUMN

It's over: spring dreams -
summer failures.   Now
we can slip on a coat more comfortable.
In autumn, no one expects much.
Just holding off winter a little longer.

Doors shut, storm windows
are installed in place of feeble screens.
You try to lift the room air conditioner
and haul it to the basement. You can
close things up now, crawl
inside your house or apartment,
under the covers. Pull
them tight around your neck.
No more sweating.

No worry about anyone calling
you to play games for a while.
All you have to do is go to work,
do the job, take the pay. Save
some for Christmas. Then
a flight south to some barbarous coast
where you have 0 degree responsibility.
You can run the beaches,
visit the bars, tell wild stories about your name.

In autumn, you can sit at a picnic table
on a good day and just stare
at her nightgown hanging
on the line next door
and imagine her in it.
You can tiptoe among pumpkins

and hardly anyone will care.
The midnight streets are prolific
with leaves you can kick like dogs
and it has been so dry they are curled
and crisp; they break under foot.

Autumn is this breaking down
of fragile things, like hopes
and illusions spawned in warmer waters.

I like it fine.

LET'S JUST SAY

Let's just say that man in the tan
Macintosh in the passenger seat of the car
that just flashed past as I stood by
the roadside waiting to cross was,
oh, Glenn Gould, or some other tall
gaunt artist in flat sunglasses and aging
or dead, say, Wallace Stevens, or
Al Purdy. Let's just say it was some older
man like that who looked at me waiting
to cross the road here in Woodstock.

Whoever it was had a sensitive face,
far too urbane for Woodstock, so
it had to be someone like that and,
if it was, I hope he was wondering
who that younger and shorter man
was and what was he doing
 in Woodstock, waiting.

ENCROACHMENT

Gracing us prior to our second shots into the first green, this fox
jogs lightly across the fairway and down
out of sight into the woods at Forest City National.
Nervous about the round until I see
this reclusive beast, my focus now winds itself
tightly around this long-legged phantom,
red and wild as D.H. Lawrence.

Our game with a ball and clubs seems tame
and slightly neurotic
in the face of a tall red fox
laughing its way into a tangled world
beyond bogies.

I have not seen many foxes and none
with legs this long. Needed,
I suppose, to run from hooks and slices.

This may be my last game,
I conclude.
There are better ways to spend time
and they have something to do with foxes.

WAS THAT YOU, JIM?

On holiday, cruising slowly the slums of my birthplace,
I see, from behind, an old man walking
down a backwater street deadending in railway tracks
and I think
this is not a good street for an old man to walk,
where the beauty has been twisted into knots.

Coming closer in my air-conditioned Taurus, I see
his bullethead crewcut on humped shoulders,
ears heavy and hairy as a pig's. He hears
the car and turns.
Grey though his unshaved jaws and shorn skull may be,
I think: that's Jim.

Jim was the brother of a close friend of mine growing up.
Considered too slow for anything productive
in those days, if still twenty today Jim could put his strength
to use in one of those workshops for our many
"specially challenged" brothers. But
all Jim did each day was head downtown
to the matinee movie, sit around the house
or walk the streets, like now. I remember
him sometimes at our school during recess
watching us play ball, but if he took a fit
his brother had to find a stick
to stop him from swallowing his tongue.
I imagine his parents were told to keep him away.

This man looks 80, who is only 60. Still,
I am surprised and glad to know he is alive,
even if sixty years of rejection make
mild monsters of men.

I consider hailing him, but don't.
He wouldn't know me and I'd be scared if he did.
Maybe all those movies were retained.
                    Anyway as I slow to a stop
Jim turns up the sidewalk to a tiny hut
with tar-paper siding and opens the screen door to go in.
Just before he enters,
looks back and waves.

  Or so I'd like this to end.

DARKNESS AND THE STAR

BEFORE THE STORM

Whiff of woodstove
lifts our heads because
it's from the wrong direction.
East wind -
storm coming.

Going home after work
we can feel it in the air,
in our bones,
in people passing.
They walk faster, faces vulnerable.
The birds have cleaned out the feeders,
the dogs are barking more,
wanting in.

The people seem resigned.
They know the work the snow
will bring, but are almost ready
to exchange extra bother
for a brief respite from routine,
some excitement in the middle
of white months.

Bring it on   the students say,
but wait until morning   so buses can't run
and school is cancelled.
A full free day in front of the tv, shoes off and popcorn..

In this neck of the woods, it seems,
storms are a part of us
that we don't exactly
  dislike.

Snow Days

i

I loved the free ride of hills
three or four to a toboggan
tearing over bumps screaming
hanging on   tipping
rolling in snow
then taking the rope in clotted mittens
and pulling the fun back up again.

ii

Or hitching rides on rear bumpers of cars, even
those old workhorses the city buses, letting them
pull you around the ancient icy streets.

iii

I loved our frozen river
stretching through the middle of town,
not dividing so much as uniting
families who skated for miles on Sundays
while we played our shining games of shinny
with twenty a side and nobody picking them
you just joined in when you got there
after putting on your skates, hands shaking
less with cold than desire to get out there
among the players.

iv

Then, for a while, life grew serious.
I did not like winters.
Dreamed of retirement
in South Carolina, somewhere alongside a marsh

or fairway: snowless final years.

v

But I have somehow reconciled with our lovely winters
and think of them now as a time I would like to suspend.
How to stretch out Christmas Eve?
You take 6 pm, I'll grab midnight
and we'll   p   u   l   l.

vi

How to crawl into a Krieghoff
and stay there
with the snow so thick
it hangs over the eaves of the farmhouse
like cupcake icing?
How to preserve the blizzards that shut our town
down for days
so you walk hip-deep up main street
and never see a car?   Everything closed
except the people, who have their feet up
by order of nature and don't feel a bit guilty
about making chili and having a big game of cards
in the middle of workday afternoon,
hoping the bloody lights go out
so we can put a match to the wicks
of coal-oil lamps and candles.

vii

How to keep with you always
the clear night sky above
as you skate on the field pond?
All those stars burning and the moon
casting diamonds everywhere on the snow
and the whole world soundless

78

except for your skates cutting
into the ice with each push of your leg.

viii

How to take these moments
and just seal them forever
in a crystal ball you can pick up and shake
ten centuries later?
The feel of cold cheeks in the night air,
the sniff of your nose trying to drip.

On The Feast Of Stephen

I like the shortest day of the year
when snow stretches like a lion
across the yards and fields
of corn stubble, two feet thick
and smooth from wind, drifting
in waves to the edge of the woods,
where a man in borrowed coats picks
up broken branches for his stove and
tosses them into a box on a sleigh.

I like the man who passes in a car
on the road who brakes to a stop,
gets out, hollers across the snow
inviting the woodsman to come with him
in his heater-warm car to his home
for soup and supper, wine and wassail.
I like this man, Stephen, who asks
into his home another creature who
does not smell good, has no manners,
and eyes the children at the table
with bitterness and a little hunger.

I like the season of giving and getting,
when children think of old men
in tattered and sooty suits
and set out cookies on plates
before they leave to go out into the night
and a winter that has just begun,
and when a horse's whinny and neighing
can barely be heard above the howls.

THIS ONE DAY

I long for the day when I can run home
to basement dark
with Christmas music and Handel,
candles and rum
and just sit at the bar like a fool,
completely free for a week or two
and immersed in the bath water
of Yuletide.
                    I yearn for this day
as I cut cane in this snake-riddled field.
I ache for darkness and the star.

ADDICTS IN GREEN

It is winter, long.

Three plants crowd
on the warm side of a large window.

Photosynthesis addicts
taking the small needles
of northern sun
every chance they get.

I see their emerald brilliance.

Wish for something
I might inject
in such certain sustenance.

Snow Tunnel to Compost Box

Now that it is deepest winter and the sun finally out,
he takes the blue plastic tool and digs a shovel-wide trench
from back deck to compost box in far corner of the yard
through two feet of igloo-perfect, brilliant blue-white snow.
It has been months of banana peels and apple cores in the garbage;
now it is time to recycle, give back.

The compost box of wooden slats is sixty feet away
as he drives the shovel down and then horizontally
under the snow wall. Then he lifts the cube and hurls it
eastward against his neighbor's fence.
Does not want it drifting back in
when the first prevailing wind kicks up.

Halfway there and panting, he sees ahead a hole
in the snow   clearly a burrow
that squirrel or rabbit has made for refuge.
It slants down to the garden he has layered with leaves
and that is where some small creature has spent
a few nights of survival.   It reminds him
of recent evenings of his own that dragged on so long
he felt half-buried himself in depression and boredom.
He has noticed a squirrel in a tree watching him
and wonders if the burrow belongs to it.
Perhaps it is still in use, so despite being in his path,
he skirts it (though no fan of squirrels) - leaves it intact
and imagines the animal grateful... such folly.

He carves his way past the fence-side lilac,
past cedar clothesline pole to the very end of the garden.
Reaching the compost box, he shovels off the lid and lifts it -
half-frozen and reluctant - then looks inside at the dry,

warmer world of leaves and teabags,

fruit and vegetable peelings, slugs and grubs

inanimate in hibernation - though perhaps

near the bottom, in the reborn dirt, they move,

taking in nourishment, carrying on

as if it were mid-summer or Florida.

He himself is one of the upper denizens:

> nearly frozen from the latter end of a life he has chosen
>
> where there is neither stimulation nor need to survive,
>
> where conversation has gone underground
>
> and the lovely flesh of young women
>
> has gone up in smoke, where the only tunnel
>
> in the house he has to return to now
>
> is a jigger of rum or some book
>
> he has signed out of the public library in desperation.

He is not at all sure whether he prefers it now

that he has reached the end of his labours,

 or that moment just before he began to dig.

BLACK ICE

Like many, I am a sucker
for details and speculations about catastrophic accidents
and their causes - unaccountable pilot error, tiny mechanical flaws.
I marvel each time I return safely
from the simplest bicycle ride,
let alone flights over ocean or mountain.

*

Turning at Harmony down a paved county road,
we were later than most traffic,
pavement bare, but deep into winter,
stars in control.
Like that perimeter strike of lightning
out of nowhere, my Camaro with its rear-
wheel drive and balding tires
began spinning 360s down the middle of the road.
In helpless awe, we watched telephone poles appear
in our windshields as we passed them in circles.
The ditches were deep,
but we twirled a tightrope right down the road's centre line.

Gravity stopped us - motor still going
and radio playing "Walking My Baby Back Home" -
in the opposite shoulder, facing the wrong way,
but ... and this is the point ... still alive
and capable of carrying on our numbered existence,
nine lives long ago spent.

We had hit black ice
on the slightest of downslopes
where on some summer Friday afternoon
a roads engineer was careless.

It was too late for traffic so we weren't killed ...

which only meant

full speed and more black ice ahead